Black Sea Regionalism:
A Case Study

Black Sea Regionalism: A Case Study

by **Andrew Robarts**

Published by the
American Historical Association
400 A Street, SE
Washington, DC 20003
www.historians.org

ABOUT THE AUTHOR

ANDREW ROBARTS is an assistant professor of Middle Eastern history at the Rhode Island School of Design. He has previously taught Middle Eastern, Ottoman, and Russian history at the University of California, Riverside and Central Connecticut State University. His book *Migration and Disease in the Black Sea Region: Ottoman-Russian Relations in the Late Eighteenth and Early Nineteenth Centuries* is forthcoming in 2016 with Bloomsbury Academic Press. Robarts has a PhD in history from Georgetown University, an MS in foreign service from Georgetown University, and a BA in history from Bowdoin College. Between his master's and PhD, Robarts worked for seven years in the refugee and humanitarian relief field for the International Rescue Committee and the United Nations High Commissioner for Refugees.

© 2015 by the American Historical Association

Cover Image: Ivan Aivazovsky, Black Sea Fleet in the Bay of Theodosia, just before the Crimean War, 1890, Aivazovsky National Art Gallery.

ISBN: 978-0-87229-209-3

Published in 2015 by the American Historical Association. As publisher, the American Historical Association does not adopt official views on any field of history and does not necessarily agree or disagree with the views expressed in this book.

Library of Congress Cataloging-in-Publication Data

Robarts, Andrew.

Black Sea regionalism: a case study / by Andrew Robarts.

p. cm. -- (Regions and Regionalisms in the Modern World)

ISBN 978-0-87229-209-3

1. Regionalism—Black Sea. I. Title.

JN98.R63 2013

327.09182'29--dc23   2013027665

Table of Contents

Regions and Regionalisms in the Modern World

Series Introduction

Regionalism is a very poorly defined and understood term in the historical literature. In part, this reflects the strong presence of methodological nationalism that dominated historical writing since the 19th century in which the nation was often the unspoken frame of reference for whichever topic was being explored. Ironically, the recent wave of globalization that has been sweeping the world since the end of the Cold War in the last decade of the 20th century, has been accompanied by an almost simultaneous process of region-formation. While this has been most obvious in the case of Europe, it has also appeared in many other parts of the world, including NAFTA in North America, Mercosur in Latin America, and in maritime Asia (ASEAN, East Asia Summit), among others. The new attention to the development of these regions has alerted many to explore the topic historically. What are the historical bases of these regions? Was there a region-making process happening under the radar during the period of high nationalism? What was the relationship of pre-modern empires to networks and connections in regions beyond their administrations? How were regions developed by modern colonial empires which were often dominated by capitalist interests who sought to integrate far flung markets? What is the relationship between globalization, regionalism and the nation-state?

By exploring these questions, the series seeks to supply some materials and concepts to grasp this neglected phenomenon suspended between national and local space and the space of globalization and world history in the modern and early modern periods in different parts of the world. The studies here investigate several key dimensions. First they distinguish regions spatially between sub-national and supra-national (or supra-state) regions. This series deals with supra-national regions, although the phenomenon of sub-national areas shaping wider regional networks is an important one.

Another important distinction refers to region-making from the bottom-up (often called regionalism) and top-down self-conscious, often ideological and political constructions of regions (sometimes called regionalization). Networks have been found to be among the most important connectors of regions, but these are not necessarily only bottom-up forces. Particularly in the modern period, the latter are subject to political and institutional requirements of territorial states which also shape them. How they negotiate these trans-border regimes is an important historical topic. While bottom-up and top-down approaches focus primarily on forces internal to the region, a third perspective foregrounds broad external processes that not only constrained and limited, but also enabled and spawned region-formation. Regions, while constituting the strategic frame of reference of historical actors, also need to be understood as entities that emerged under the pressures of the international state-system and capitalist integration. In this reading, regionalisms are not only based on shared characteristics, and are not made entirely from within, but are also responses to forces from without and to larger processes of global integration.

Related to these topics is another set of analytical questions: what is the role of economic forces in relation to social, cultural and religious networks? When do political and military contests erupt to control a region? This question rose sharply and devastatingly in World War II when the Germans sought to create a European region under their control and the Japanese sought to do so in East Asia. Finally, there is the matter of cultural regions and their relationship to political and economic factors in creating an identity in a region. Can regions remain spaces of imagination for diverse and heterogeneous groups in a way that the nation is not?

Lastly, we know that historically geography has been a necessary but not sufficient condition for a region. One of the aims of this series is to tackle this tension between physical constraints and the constructed character of the region. Among the factors that have facilitated trans-regional connections and networks, producing regional imaginaries and practices that define the extension of the region, is technology. In the networked and super-speed world of contemporary society is the physical region relevant at all? We believe that physical forms which cross national boundaries—rivers, forests, ecologies, ocean currents—not only remain important, but have become more so as humans have accelerated their degradation and depletion. The regions that have been shaped by this geography—beyond nations—will have to respond to this threat collectively or regionally.

—*Sebastian Conrad and Prasenjit Duara*
Series Editors

Introduction

The economic and political cycles of the Black Sea region have fluctuated between periods dominated by a closed command economy and periods marked by international openness and free trade. Between the 15th and 18th centuries, the political economy of the Black Sea region was organized around the monopolistic provisioning of the Ottoman capital of Istanbul. Non-Ottoman or non-Ottoman-flagged trading vessels were prohibited from engaging in commerce on the Black Sea.[1] At the start of the modern era, a series of treaties and trade agreements signed by the Ottoman and Russian Empires initiated a long period in the history of the Black Sea region that, in its relative openness, commercial activity, and demographic exchange, resembled the "glory days" of the Black Sea region from the 13th through 15th centuries. In this comparison, the Russians play the role of the Mongols (a strong political entity established on the northern shore of the Black Sea and its hinterland); the Ottomans play the role of the Byzantines (a stable empire established on the straits of the Bosporus and Dardanelles); and the British, French, and Austrians play the role of the Italian city-states (European states engaged, politically and economically, in the Black Sea region).[2] Following a period of closure during the Cold War era, the 20 years since the collapse of the Soviet Union have seen the return of the Black Sea region to full participation in the international system.

Defining a region as "a distinct geographical zone of interaction," Charles King has identified migrants and merchants as the main connective tissues linking the communities and polities in the Black Sea basin. Through periods of openness and closure, and regardless of shifts in political power, trading and migrant communities in the Black Sea basin forged and sustained trans-national and -regional connections. As King writes, "even during those times when the sea has been a zone of confrontation, it has remained a region: a unique playing field on which the interests and aspirations of the peoples and polities within it have been played out. Interactions, exchanges, and connections—sometimes peaceful, sometimes conflictual—have been the defining elements around the sea's shores."[3]

A historical analysis of intra-regional relations (economic, political, social, and cultural) around the Black Sea basin can provide a useful frame of reference for researchers and teachers looking to contextualize issues in the region today. These issues include ecological degradation and environmentalism, the construction of oil and natural gas pipelines, irregular migration, arms smuggling, human trafficking, terrorism, and the emergence of a Russian-Turkish condominium over the region's political and economic affairs. Although the Black Sea region does not have as developed a political formation or structure as do the North American Free Trade Agreement (NAFTA) countries, the Association of Southeast Asian Nations (ASEAN), or Mercosur in South America, regional ties and cooperation will continue to characterize and underpin relations among countries and societies in the Black Sea basin.[4]

Through an integrative analysis of local, communal, and global processes, this manuscript addresses the dynamics of the Black Sea region from a world-historical perspective, and provides a theoretical framework within which to examine inter-state and inter-societal relations in the region today. The manuscript is divided into four sections. It begins with an overview of the region and offers a conceptualization of Black Sea regionalism that draws upon the theory and principles of New Regionalism. Following an outline of Black Sea organizations and the cultural, economic, and political projects undertaken by these organizations (the totality of which I call the "architecture" of the Black Sea region), the second section poses one of the central questions for this region (and for regional studies in general): are regions mainly and merely imagined constructs, or can a region (in both its geographic and political expression) be identified and defined through empirically based research and analysis? Section three takes up this question and, through a discussion of historical breaks and continuities in the Black Sea region in the modern period, offers a conceptual and empirical framework within which to analyze Black Sea regionalism in the early part of the 21st century. This analysis of breaks and continuities in the history of Black Sea regionalism focuses, at the political and state levels, on relations among western European countries, Russia, and Turkey in the Black Sea region. At the social and cultural level, the formation and articulation of diaspora communities in the Black Sea region and smuggling and human-trafficking activity in the Black Sea region are highlighted. Here the central role of the state-migrant nexus in the formation of Black Sea regionalism (both historically and today) is analyzed. Section three closes with a discussion on environmentalism and international security interests in the Black Sea region. Drawing on the case study developed in the preceding three sections, the fourth and final section identifies potential challenges that lie ahead for scholars of regionalism, and speculates on the future prospects of this burgeoning analytical field.

An Overview of the Black Sea Region and Black Sea Regionalism

As wielded by politicians, journalists, and analysts, the term "region" can be slippery and elastic. The term has been applied expansively to such geographic areas as the Middle East, the North Atlantic, or the Arctic, and applied narrowly to define a metropolitan area or a province. In the context of the Black Sea, a narrow conceptualization of the region would cover the 16 million people who live along the Black Sea coast and its immediate hinterland.[5] A more expansive understanding of the region (or what is commonly referred to as "the Wider Black Sea Region" or "the Greater Black Sea Region") would cover the 160 to 170 million people who live along the lower courses of the Danube, Dnieper, and Don Rivers (the second, third, and fourth longest rivers in Europe), which collectively form most of the Black Sea drainage basin. Several international organizations (including the International Organization for Migration, or IOM) describe the region as covering an area of 20 million square kilometers and hosting a population of an estimated 350 million people.[6] Charles King avoids population figures and statistical measurements, demarcating the region instead as the "land- and seascape from the Balkans to the Caucasus and from the Ukrainian and Russian steppe to Anatolia."[7]

As with most with regions, the character and scope of the Black Sea region depends in large measure on the perspective taken and the issues addressed. The widening of one's analytical lens to include noncoastal states (i.e. the wider Black Sea region) significantly expands the security-related dimension in Black Sea affairs. Here, two frozen conflicts (Armenia and Azerbaijan over Nagorno-Karabakh and Russia and Moldova over Transnistria) as well as the on-again off-again animosity between Turkey and Greece are added to the regional equation.[8]

As a counterpoint to this security or geopolitically driven lens, the principles of "New Regionalism" offer a more socially, culturally, and environmentally oriented understanding of Black Sea regionalism. According to Pertti Joenniemi, New Regionalism points to an "ostensibly de-politicized version of regionality, where politics ranks much lower than economics, environment, communication, and technology." The concepts of New Regionalism valorize forces that challenge sovereignty, transcend hierarchies, cross borders, promote regional cooperation, bridge political divides, and are spontaneous, impulsive, and inclusive. In a region where these types of forces prevail, security concerns are downgraded and diversity, variance, decentralization, and fragmentation are tolerated.[9] In a regional formation influenced by the dynamics and mechanics of New Regionalism, differences in national units are elided to form solidarities across boundaries.[10]

The potential saliency of New Regionalism in the Black Sea region lies in the provision of a more comfortable and less historically or politically freighted form of regional identity and civic participation. This liberating form of regionalism has the potential to blur contentious dividing lines between those Black Sea states that are members of a specific international military, economic, or political association (i.e. Bulgaria and Romania in the European Union and Bulgaria, Romania, and Turkey in NATO) and those who are not (i.e. Ukraine, Russia, and Georgia). Finally, and perhaps most importantly, new Black Sea regionalism offers the potential for a less politicized form of communal identity and a variant of intersocietal interaction based not on religion, language, ethnicity, or nationality.[11]

In terms of methodology, the history of maritime spaces guides my analysis of Black Sea regionalism.[12] Adopting a transnational perspective, Charles King argues that the Black Sea, like bodies of water in general, has traditionally acted more like a bridge than a barrier to exchange and communication between peoples and societies established on the northern and southern shores of the Black Sea.[13] And Eyüp Özveren has concluded that "not only Odessa on the Russian coast but also Trabzon on the Ottoman side, a historical port-city located on long-distance trade routes, rose to primacy once port-city networks started to integrate the Black Sea world."[14] By extension, one can make the argument that in the context of the Black Sea region the societies and economies of key port-cities around the Black Sea (the list of which would include—in addition to Odessa and Trabzon—Constanta, Romania; Varna and Burgas, Bulgaria; and, of course, Istanbul, Turkey) have more in common with each other than they do with communities in their respective "national" hinterlands. In short, maritime spaces promote the historicity of space through the structural contingency of relationships among cultures and peoples.[15]

The Architecture of Black Sea Regionalism

There are many regionalist projects currently underway around the Black Sea basin. Looking at the goals of these projects, as well as the regionalist terminology employed by various Black Sea organizations and associations, one can certainly *imagine* that a Black Sea region exists. Determining whether the activities undertaken by these organizations have any resonance for the communities and individuals around the Black Sea littoral, however, is more difficult. How integrated is the early 21st-century Black Sea region politically, economically, and culturally? It is to these questions that the manuscript now turns.

At the macroeconomic and international levels, early 21st-century Black Sea regionalism is by and large a state-driven project "designed to re-organize a particular regional space along defined economic and political lines."[16] As Leo Ching has noted, the globalization of capital has reduced barriers for economic exchange and created the space for the elaboration of dynamic, integrated, and economically driven regional associations. Indeed it can be argued that in the context of the Black Sea region over the course of the last 20 years a region previously defined by ideological and military confrontation has given way to one of increasing economic cooperation and integration.

Founded in 1992, the Organization of the Black Sea Economic Cooperation (BSEC) is the grandfather of all early 21st-century Black Sea organizations. The stated goals of the BSEC are to foster economic and political harmony among member states, and to promote good-neighborly relations. At its core, the operations of the BSEC are driven by a "belief in the utility of regional cooperation as a basis of enhanced stability and security."[17] The BSEC currently has 12 member states (the littoral states of Russia, Ukraine, Romania, Georgia, Bulgaria, and Turkey, plus Albania, Azerbaijan, Armenia, Greece, Moldova, and Serbia) and purports to speak for and represent the interests of 350 million people. The wide-ranging areas of inter-state and -regional cooperation cited in the BSEC's literature include combating crime, promoting tourism, protecting the environment, and improving Black Sea infrastructure. The BSEC helps organize the Olympic-style Black Sea Games (which were held in Trabzon, Turkey, in 2007; Constanta, Romania, in 2010; and Samsun, Turkey, in 2014) and has proclaimed October 31 to be International Black Sea Day.

Organizations affiliated with the BSEC include the Black Sea Trade and Development Bank (established in Thessaloniki, Greece, in 1999 to focus on economic development, trade, regional cooperation, and the economic integration of the Black Sea region) and the International Centre for Black Sea Studies (founded in Athens, Greece, in 1998, to serve as a think-tank devoted to regional policy and research). Other policy and politically oriented Black Sea organizations operating at the intergovernmental level include the Atlantic Council, which convenes the annual Black Sea Energy & Economic Forum (a high-level gathering of influential and senior government and private-sector leaders) and focuses on regional economic cooperation, energy security, investment, trade, and developing the idea of community in the greater Black Sea area; and the Blue Black Sea International Congress on Politics, Economics, and Society, dedicated to regional cooperation and the resolution of frozen conflicts in the wider Black Sea region.

Although a regional consciousness based on the cultural solidarity and historical unity of peoples and societies in the Black Sea basin is not as well developed as the technical aspects of state-driven Black Sea regionalism, there are a variety of organizations devoted to promoting a culturally identifiable "supranational regionalist imaginary" and promoting a regional cultural idiom among the societies and peoples of the Black Sea region.[18] The Black Sea Trust for Regional Cooperation is one of these organizations, operated by the German Marshall Fund to "foster regional and cross-border ties in the public, private, and non-profit sectors, seeding the development of a thriving civil society and a cohesive regional identity that bonds the countries of the wider region to each other and to the countries of the transatlantic community." Another is the Black Sea-Caspian Sea International Fund, founded in Bucharest in 2009 to strengthen regional cooperation in economic, environmental, health care, educational, and cultural matters. The International Black Sea Club, founded in 1992, promotes cooperation among port-cities on the Black and Mediterranean Seas through a focus on ecology, tourism, and cultural exchange, and the Black Sea Universities Network coordinates common research and training projects among 53 Black Sea-based universities.

In the modern period, the impulse to regionalism can be viewed as part of the ongoing and persistent desire by certain segments of society to transcend the nation-state. Therefore, while the current articulation of regionalism in the Black Sea basin is primarily a state-driven project, it is important to note that at both the popular and societal levels regional formations in the Black Sea basin can and have often taken on an organic dimension. Coalescing around the conceptualization of a shared regional history, this organic form of regionalism has been driven by ideational exchange, promoted through cultural interaction, and sustained by intra-regional migration among littoral communities and societies. Across history, the geographic immutability of the Black Sea region has sustained and promoted the vitality of transnational forces. In the *longue durée*, the Black Sea region evinces a quantifiable and empirically verifiable pattern of exchange and interaction that has both challenged and weakened the territorial sovereignty of empires and nation-states.

To date, very little effort has been made by Black Sea states and societies to stimulate political action by linking diverse local histories to a larger (or regional) historical narrative.[19] Black Sea organizations and the projects they undertake rarely refer to (or draw upon) any real or imagined regional history, in part because "numerous case studies and monographs remain within the narrow confines of the many national languages. Hence, linguistic diversity has served not only to divide the Black Sea world culturally but also to distort the existing body of literature in favor of nation-state oriented histories."[20] The opportunity exists, therefore, for the elaboration of a history of Black Sea regionalism that—through the identification and promotion of a shared regional history—stimulates and deepens the economic and political integration of the Black Sea region.

Historical Continuities in Black Sea Regionalism

"As we consider this rapid review of the broader currents of history, does not a certain persistence of geographical relationship become evident?"

Halford Mackinder, *The Geographical Pivot of History*

In this section I identify and analyze historical breaks and continuities in Black Sea regionalism and discuss the emergent mechanisms and new trajectories that have the potential to generate a regional formation in the Black Sea basin going forward in the 21st century. This analysis draws primarily upon a historical and contemporary discussion of the centrality of Russian-Turkish relations in the Black Sea region and is focused on diplomatic, geopolitical, and ideologically driven breaks and continuities in the history of Black Sea regionalism. Following this politically oriented discussion of inter-state relations in the Black Sea region, I move to an analysis of the social dimension in Black Sea regionalism. Here long-standing regional processes and reoccurring features of Black Sea regionalism are discussed, including the formation and articulation of diaspora communities in the Black Sea region as well as smuggling and human-trafficking activities in the Black Sea basin. Promoted by environmental and structural factors, the interplay between migratory populations and state-driven policies geared towards controlling or managing these populations has been an enduring component of Black Sea regionalism. Therefore, this section—while highlighting breaks in the political history of Black Sea regionalism—emphasizes the durability of the state-migration nexus and the continuity of migration-generated regionalism in the Black Sea basin, both historically and today. Under the rubric of new trajectories in contemporary Black Sea regionalism, this section closes with an analysis of the potential role for environmental activism in galvanizing regional action in the Black Sea basin and the ways in which the external and security-related objectification of the Black Sea region could hasten, provoke, and stimulate regional formations in the Black Sea basin in the 21st century. To what extent have regional ties survived and shaped the Black Sea region today? And to what extent is the Black Sea region a new

creation, produced under the impact of global interaction? It is to these two
questions that this manuscript now turns.

European, Russian, and Ottoman (Turkish) Relations in the Black Sea Region

When addressing the Black Sea region, Euro-Atlantic historians and
political analysts tend to focus on the trilateral relationship among western
Europe, Russia, and Turkey. Within this framework, historians and analysts
typically emphasize western European influence on the Ottoman Empire's
adoption of modernizing reforms in the 19th century and debate the depth
and impact of European contributions to Russia's historical trajectory.
Political analysts expend considerable energy discussing the pros and cons
of Turkey's admission into the European Union and focus on the (often)
testy relationship between the Russian Federation and the European Union
and NATO. This emphasis on European-Russian and European-Turkish
relations (both historical and contemporary) elides and undersells the
most important dimension of political and economic affairs in the Black
Sea region—the relationship between Turkey and Russia. This relationship
has deep historical roots and will have the most influence on the nature of
economic and political affairs in the Black Sea region in the 21st century.

For example, according to conventional historiography, in the 1840s
the Ottoman Empire—under pressure from western Europe—called upon
European experts to provide technical assistance and guidance in drafting
policies and regulations to check the spread of disease in the Ottoman
Empire. However, prior to the 1840s, the Ottoman and Russian states
had already undertaken joint efforts to check the spread of disease across
the Black Sea region through the imposition of stern anti-disease measures
on infected populations and the creation of new institutions of border
and social control. The regional dimension of the Ottoman and Russian
response to external and internal security threats must be addressed in
conjunction with any discussion on the international (or western European)
contributions to modernizing reforms in the Ottoman Empire. Indeed, as
Eyüp Özveren contends, in the context of Turkish-Russian relations in the
Black Sea region "periodic outbursts of hostilities between the two empires
should, nevertheless, not obscure the relations of give and take as well as of
impact and response from the viewpoint of progress towards modernity."[21]

In the late 18th century (following the signing of the Ottoman-Russian
Treaty of Küçük Kaynarca in 1774) the Black Sea region developed into
an active zone of exchange between the Ottoman and Russian Empires.
The two key regional characteristics of the Black Sea basin—commercial

interaction and large-scale migration—linked these two powerful empires along a clearly defined north-south axis and the Russian and Ottoman Empires enjoyed a duopoly over political and economic affairs in the Black Sea region. This continuity was disrupted, starting in the 1830s, by the internationalization of affairs in the Black Sea region. This disruption can be dated to the signing of the Ottoman-Russian Treaty of Hünkar Iskelesi in 1833. A mutual defense agreement between the Ottoman and Russian Empires, the Treaty of Hünkar Iskelesi alerted France and Britain to the Russian Empire's improved diplomatic and military position in Istanbul. The ensuing internationalization of the "Black Sea Question" effectively ended a 60-year Ottoman-Russian duopoly over economic and political affairs in the Black Sea region.

The key historical factors and events that promoted and sustained the primacy of extra-regional influences on the political trajectory of the 19th- and early 20th-century Black Sea region include the promulgation of a series of international conventions governing access to the Black Sea via the straits of the Bosporus and Dardanelles; the convening of numerous international sanitary conferences to discuss ways to check the spread of disease from the Ottoman Empire to Europe; the British and French occupation of the Crimean Peninsula during the Crimean War of 1853–56; and the terms of the Treaty of Berlin in 1878 (signed following the conclusion of the Russo-Ottoman War of 1877–78), which effectively established the political boundaries of the modern Black Sea region.

In addition to the post-1830s internationalization of the Black Sea region, the Ottoman-Russian duopoly over political and economic affairs in the Black Sea basin—which had been the defining feature of Black Sea regionalism in the late 18th and early 19th centuries—suffered an additional rupture as a result of a growing religious and nationalist-inspired ideological schism between the Ottoman and Russian Empires in the second half of the 19th century. Driven by increasingly shrill expressions of pan-Slavic and pan-Turkic solidarity across the Black Sea region, this schism was fanned by the irredentist imperial propaganda of the Ottoman Sultan Abdülhamid II (1876–1909) that was largely directed towards the sizable Muslim population in the Russian Empire, and the pro-Slavic propaganda of Tsarist officials in Moscow and Istanbul that was largely directed towards Slavic-Orthodox populations in the Ottoman Balkans.

Russian efforts to regulate the sizable annual pilgrimage (*Hajj*) of Russian Muslims to the Holy Lands of Mecca and Medina via the Black Sea and Istanbul typified this shift to an ideological and religious orientation in the political affairs of the region.[22] Links between Russian Muslim communities,

Tatar populations in Istanbul, and Islamic scholars in the Hejaz, as well as the pan-Islamic ideas that spread along the *Hajj* routes between the Russian Empire and the Hejaz via the Ottoman Empire posed a distinct threat, in the minds of imperial administrators, to the Russian Empire's territorial integrity.[23] Forced migrants from the Russian Empire frequently sought refuge in the Hejaz, and for many Central Asian *Hajjis* the pilgrimage to Mecca and Medina was not complete without an extended stay in Istanbul.[24] Tatar student associations formed in Istanbul, and by 1909 a Scholarly Association of Muslim Students from Russia materialized in Mecca to assist in the religious instruction of Russian Muslim students, intending that they return to the Russian Empire ready to pass along knowledge gained from their time in Mecca.[25]

Freedom to engage in the *Hajj*, which Catherine the Great had granted to Russia's Muslims in the 1773 Edict of Tolerance, had by the second half of the 19th century come under increasing attack by Russian imperial administrators concerned with the spread of pan-Islamic ideology among the empire's Muslim populations. Increasingly in the second half of the 19th century, Russian officials advocated the prohibition of travel to Mecca, and the adoption of measures to counteract anti-Christian ideas bred by connections between the Muslim population in the Russian Empire and scholars and students in the Hejaz.[26] For Russian Muslims in the second half of the 19th century, "the pilgrimage to Mecca remained a contested right."[27] The late 19th-century religious schism between the Russian and Ottoman Empires dissipated in the wake of World War I with the empires' collapse and their replacement by the communist Soviet Union and secular Republic of Turkey.

While late 19th- and early 20th-century political elites and state actors promoted meta-political concepts such as pan-Turkism, pan-Slavism, and nationalism, at the local or social level ideological and/or religious differences tended to be sublimated to more communal concerns. Indeed, well into the early 20th century, travelers and political anthropologists expecting to find homogenous national groupings in the region were surprised to find "individuals and communities for whom plural identities and mixed cultures were the norm."[28] Following the Crimean War, many segments of Russian society in the Crimean Peninsula were sympathetic to the plight of their Crimean Tatar neighbors and sought to prevent their out-migration to the Ottoman Empire. Little overt antagonism existed on the grassroots level between the Slavic population of the Crimea and the local Tatars, who had "long been used to the sound of church bells."[29] Going forward into the 21st century, the historical dissipation of meta-political narratives at the local level, and the continuity in this phenomenon throughout the region's micro-history, increases the likelihood for a more communal or socially articulated form of regionalism in the Black Sea basin.

Just as the primacy of Russian-Turkish relations in Black Sea regional dynamics emerged in the late 18th century, so has the Russian-Turkish-oriented regionality in Black Sea affairs re-emerged in the 20 years since the collapse of the Soviet Union and the Cold War closure of the Black Sea region. Russia and Turkey's economic and political interests in the region in the early 21st century are complementary. Turkey conducts more trade with Russia than it does with any other country, and roughly 70 percent of the natural gas consumed in Turkey is sourced from Russia. Turkish businessmen and corporations are particularly active in the Black Sea region and have captured a large portion of the regional economic market, particularly in the construction and engineering sectors. Over 25 percent of the profits earned by Turkish construction and engineering firms come from projects in the former Soviet Union. And Turkish construction companies grabbed a sizable chunk of the US$10 billion allotted for construction for Sochi 2014.[30] Russia and Turkey both opposed America's invasion and occupation of Iraq and see eye-to-eye on minimizing the projection of US military power in the Black Sea region. Despite its status as a member of NATO, Turkey's moderated response to the Russian invasion of Georgia in 2008 typifies the rapprochement between Turkey and Russia on the region's military affairs.

The signing in May 2010 of an extensive trade and energy agreement between Turkey and Russia demonstrates the enduring strength of the relationship between these two regional powers. In this agreement, Russia and Turkey agreed to lift visa requirements for tourists travelling between the two countries. Russian and Turkish ministers also discussed the formation of a joint airline company and initiated negotiations on the construction of a Russian-made nuclear power plant in southern Turkey.[31] The possibility does exist—with Russian Prime Minister Vladimir Putin's neo-imperialist impulses and the Islamist politics espoused by Turkish Prime Minister Tayyip Erdoğan—for a re-emergence of an ideological schism between Russian and Turkey in the Black Sea region.[32] However, for now, economic and political considerations will more than likely continue to trump any latent ideological or religious schisms between Russia and Turkey. This continuity in the Russian-Turkish condominium over the trajectory of political and economic affairs in the Black Sea region carries with it the potential for a more coherent and unitary expression of Black Sea regionalism. In sum, while not discounting occasional bouts of geo-strategic and ideological confrontation between Russia and Turkey, any discussion of the history of Black Sea regionalism must emphasize the "transnational" character of

Russian-Turkish relations in the Black Sea region—both historically and today.

Migration and the Articulation of Diaspora Communities in the Black Sea Region

Large-scale population movements, shifting patterns of agricultural settlement, and the commercial and political activities of migrant diasporas animated and energized the Black Sea world in the 19th and early 20th century. Today, trade, return migration, and intra-communal communications around the Black Sea littoral continue to forge strong and enduring structural connections among migrant communities in the region. My goal here is to demonstrate how the process of diaspora formation—through the establishment of regional communication networks and historically high rates of return migration—contributed in the past and will continue to contribute in the future to socially constructed and culturally articulated expressions of Black Sea regionalism.

A short and by no means exhaustive inventory of the "ethnic" and religious populations on the move throughout the region in the 19th and early 20th century would include Armenians, Greeks, Wallachians, Moldovans, Gagauz, Gypsies, Cossacks, and Russian Old Believers. In terms of numbers, Bulgarians and Crimean Tatars constituted two of the largest groups of migratory populations in the modern history of the Black Sea region. Over 250,000 Bulgarians (or 10–15 percent of the total Bulgarian population in the Ottoman Empire) migrated from the Ottoman Balkans to the Danubian Principalities (modern-day Romania) and southern Russia in the period between 1768 and the mid-19th century.

As Ottoman allies or vassals since the early 1400s, the Crimean Tatars established significant diaspora communities on the territory of the Ottoman Empire. Alan Fisher estimates that between the outbreak of the Russo-Turkish War of 1768–74 and the Treaty of Jassy in 1792, from 150,000 to 200,000 Crimean Tatars out-migrated from the Russian Empire.[33] Brian Williams argues that in the first few decades of the 19th century, a quiet and steady migration took of tens of thousands of Crimean Tatar peasants from the Russian to the Ottoman Empire. Historians are in general agreement on an estimate of between 200,000 to 250,000 Crimean Tatar and Nogay refugees fleeing the Russian Empire for the Ottoman Empire during and after the Crimean War (1853–56).[34] In the latter half of the 19th century and early part of the 20th, well over one million Russian Muslims immigrated to the Ottoman Empire.[35] Kemal Karpat estimates that between 1829 and 1914, five to seven million Muslims (including

Crimean Tatars, Nogay Tatars, and Circassians) were "forced" to migrate from the Russian Empire and settle in the Ottoman Empire.[36]

This migration of Tatars from the Russian to the Ottoman Empires after the conclusion of the Crimean War was just one of the many large scale population movements in the Black Sea region in the second half of the 19th century. These migrations contributed to a significant population increase along the Black Sea coast in the late 19th century. By the second half of the 19th century, the population of Varna (the largest Bulgarian city on the Black Sea coast) had risen to 40,000, and the population of the Russian Black Sea port of Nikolaev had tripled in size. In this same period, the populations of the Russian Black Sea port-cities of Odessa and Rostov grew six-fold and ten-fold, respectively. According to Charles King, the collapse of the Russian and Ottoman Empires and the post-World War I settlement of political boundaries in the region sparked a "series of massive population movements that dwarfed the multiple exoduses of the late 19th century."[37]

Following a 20th-century interlude from World War I to the dissolution of the Soviet Union, high levels of in- and out-migration have re-emerged as a key structural component in Black Sea regionalism. Indeed, the size and saliency of structural migration in the region at the start of the 21st century has led Charles King to conclude that "the population movements of the 1990s and the early 2000s—the flow of economic migrants, asylum-seekers, transit migrants and refugees—may yet transform the demographic structure of the region in as profound a way as the region's last major period of mass population movements: the multiple rounds of ethnic cleansing and war-time displacement that took place from the 1860s and the 1920s."[38]

In general, historical scholarship on the region's migration patterns emphasizes a one-way flow of migratory movements from one Black Sea country to another. Approaching the question of migration in the region through the prism of nationalist and/or Cold War historiography, this scholarship tends to highlight the paternal role played by the Russian and Ottoman states in providing a safe haven for Slavic-Orthodox and Muslim populations fleeing the tyranny of Ottoman and Russian oppression. This scholarship overlooks the significant amount of Slavic-Orthodox *return* migration from the Russian Empire to the Ottoman Empire in the early part of the 19th century, and the significant amount of Tatar and Muslim *return* migration from the Ottoman Empire to the Russian Empire in the second half of the 19th century. Return migration, non-linear migration, circular migration, frequent in- and out-migration, and multiple secondary moves typify population movements in the Black Sea region, both historically and today.

In the first decades of the 19th century, a significant number of Bulgarian settlers in southern Russia opted to return to the Ottoman Empire. Many of these return migrations occurred after only a short stay in the Russian Empire. Reports filed by Ottoman provincial governors in the Balkans attest to the generalized nature of Bulgarian return migration to the Ottoman Empire in the early 1830s. From 1833–34, an estimated 20,000 Bulgarians engaged in return migrations from southern Russia to the Ottoman Empire.[39] In the period from 1861–83, 10,000 Crimean Tatars who had fled from the Russian to the Ottoman Empire after the conclusion of the Crimean War applied for and were granted passports to return to the Russian Empire. Throughout the rest of the 19th century and into the early part of the 20th, Crimean Tatar and other Muslim migratory groups continued to return in significant numbers to the Russian Empire following brief stays in the Ottoman Empire. Many of these Crimean Tatar émigrés managed to obtain and retain subjecthood in both the Ottoman and Russian Empires.[40] This "dual-citizenship" status eased population movements around the Black Sea region and diluted attempts by the Ottoman and Russian Empires to impose territorial sovereignty in the Black Sea basin.

In the Black Sea region connections among migrant communities have endured despite ongoing efforts by Black Sea states—through the erection of treaty-defined border lines and the imposition of travel documentation regimes—to establish territorial sovereignty. In the modern period, the overall effectiveness of administrative, bureaucratic, and technological innovations (such as quarantines and travel documentation regimes) adopted by the Ottoman and Russian states to improve the management of migratory populations crisscrossing the Black Sea region has been minimal at best. According to James Meyer, in the 19th century "Russian Muslims were not simply categorized and shaped by these regulations but also engaged them and found loopholes through which they could pursue personal advantage. Like Armenians, Greeks, and Jews, and others traveling between the two empires, Russian Muslims frequently devised strategies that helped them take advantage of the categorical ambiguity of their positions. Living as Russians in the Ottoman Empire and Ottomans in Russia, these individuals succeeded in manipulating the politics of citizenship on both sides of the frontier."[41]

Despite the best efforts of Russian and Turkish state servitors and border guards, migrants on the move in the Black Sea region in the 19th century were aware of, and sought out, the easiest points of entry into the Ottoman and Russian Empires. In the fall of 1830 Russian officials posted along the

Danubian border between Ottoman Bulgaria and Wallachia (Romania) received reports of a significant drop in Bulgarian migrant arrivals at the Kalaraşi quarantine station (across the Danube River from the Bulgarian city of Silistra) and a significant increase in migrant arrivals at the Braila and Pioa Pietri quarantine stations (at the head of the Danubian estuary).[42] The result of a shorter quarantine period and less stringent documentation requirements in Braila and Pioa Pietri as compared to those in force in Kalaraşi, this shift in the Bulgarian migratory pattern—as a counter to recently enacted Russian border security measures—typifies the fluidity in the state-migrant nexus in the Black Sea region, both historically and today.

The breadth of communication and information exchange among Black Sea diasporas and migratory communities contributed to the high and sustained level of migration in the Black Sea region and further frustrated efforts by Black Sea states to effectively manage migration around the basin. In the 19th century, members of Bulgarian migrant communities in the Black Sea region communicated with their kinsmen about the pros and cons of settlement conditions in the Russian Empire and the Ottoman Balkans. Information obtained in this manner often convinced Bulgarians in the Ottoman Empire to take their chances and seek material improvement through migration to southern Russia.[43] Conversely, word of favorable economic and resettlement conditions in the Ottoman Balkans in the period after the Russo-Ottoman War of 1828–29, stimulated considerable Bulgarian return migration to the Ottoman Empire.[44] According to Brian Williams, Tatar diasporas in the Ottoman Balkans and Anatolia were in regular communication with Tatar populations remaining in the Crimea. And Kemal Karpat argues that word of the positive reception and treatment of Crimean Tatars in the Ottoman Empire after the Crimean War acted as a classic migration magnet and encouraged higher levels of Crimean Tatar in-migration to the Ottoman Empire.[45]

Historically, the depth and intensity of diasporic communication in the Black Sea region has had important political implications. The intellectual and economic contributions of diaspora communities to the cause of national liberation movements in the Ottoman Empire in the 19th century cannot be underestimated. Leading figures in the sizable Bulgarian diaspora community in Istanbul provided crucial political leadership to the cause of Bulgarian national liberation in the mid-19th century, and Bulgarian merchant communities in Odessa and Bucharest contributed, logistically and materially, to armed nationalist uprisings in Bulgaria in the 1860s and 1870s.[46] The *Philiki Eteria* (a Greek revolutionary society established in 1814) drew its membership and financial support from the large and influential Greek diaspora community in Odessa. The political and military activities of the *Philiki Eteria* are generally credited with having initiated the Greek War of Independence against Ottoman Turkish rule in the 1820s and 1830s.[47]

The formation and articulation of diaspora communities and their ability to circumvent efforts by Black Sea states to enforce political and territorial sovereignty continues to be a key characteristic of the state-migrant nexus in the Black Sea region today. Turkish businessmen and traders have established themselves in Odessa, while Ukrainian migrants and settlers have formed a visible community in Istanbul. The Chechen diaspora along the Bulgarian coast controls a large segment of the lucrative Black Sea tourist industry in Bulgaria. Statistics compiled by the IOM document the migratory links among countries around the Black Sea littoral and the ongoing dispersion of peoples in the Black Sea region. Annually, an estimated 13.6 million migrants are on the move in the Black Sea basin. According to the IOM, intra-regional migration accounts for roughly 60 percent of total immigration into Black Sea countries. Russia is the primary source country for intra-regional migration, accounting for 22.5 percent of intra-regional migrants. Moldova, Georgia, Ukraine, Bulgaria, and Romania all send a large number of labor migrants to Russia and Turkey.[48] These regional migration flows remained relatively stable throughout the first decade of the 21st century.

Building on these migration statistics, figures documenting the increase of remittances returned to home countries testify to the enduring vibrancy and interconnectedness of diaspora communities in the Black Sea basin. According to the World Bank, in 2007 the countries of the Black Sea region exchanged US$26.7 billion in remittances—a 150 percent increase over remittance data collected in 2000. According to the IOM, "the actual amount including unrecorded flows through formal and informal channels is believed to be significantly larger." With the exception of Greece and Turkey, all Black Sea countries experienced an increase in remittances provided by regional migrants in the period from 2000 to 2007. Romania is estimated to have received US$6.8 billion in remittances in 2007, making it the 10th largest recipient of remittances in the world. In Moldova, remittances accounted for 36.2 percent of the country's GDP, making it (together with Tajikistan) the world's largest recipient of remittances as a percentage of GDP. In Bulgaria and Georgia, over 50 percent of migrant remittances are returned to home families and communities via "informal channels." Most funds remitted to home countries are transported by migrants personally or by friends and acquaintances. In Georgia, for instance, "friends travelling home" handled 35 percent of the country's remittances in 2007.[49]

As has been the case throughout the history of the Black Sea region, the dynamism of migratory flows in the Black Sea region continues—at one and the same time—to knit the Black Sea together and erode the sovereignty of nation-states around the Black Sea littoral. Intra-regional connections forged by diasporic communication networks and systems of exchange coupled with high rates of return migration in the Black Sea basin have and will more than likely continue to promote the articulation and expression of a regionally based identity among individuals, littoral societies, and coastal communities in the Black Sea region.

Smuggling and Human Trafficking in the Black Sea Region

Uncontrolled migration and the collateral (and illegal) phenomenon of smuggling and human-trafficking activity in the Black Sea region promotes the adoption of state-driven and technically oriented regionalist policies among Black Sea states. Desirous of controlling the movements of migratory populations but struggling to effectively manage migration in the Black Sea region, Black Sea states (primarily Russia and Turkey) have periodically, from the early 19th century onward—even during periods of geopolitical and ideological conflict—pursued a regional response to uncontrolled migration.[50]

Throughout history, freebooters of all types, ethnicities, and denominations have pursued their fortunes in the Black Sea region. According to Charles King, in the early part of the 19th century, Bessarabia (the area between the Dniester and Prut Rivers or roughly modern-day Moldova) became "a haven for smugglers and other criminals operating along the Danube and the Black Sea."[51] Expert in navigating the coastal waters of the northwestern Black Sea coast, smugglers and pirates easily evaded Ottoman and Russian quarantine facilities, operating beyond the detection of provincial and port authorities. Assigned to peacetime duty in southern Russia, Zaporozhian Cossacks bootlegged black-market goods through ports in the Danubian delta. Around the Black Sea basin in the late 18th and early 19th centuries, military conflict, political rivalry, and the physical and psychological dislocation associated with migration challenged individuals' sense of loyalty and promoted the adoption of new identities.

Trafficking in human cargo was a lucrative business in the Black Sea region in the 19th century. In return for cash payments, bands of Zaporozhian Cossacks organized the clandestine transportation of Bulgarian migrants between Ottoman- and Russian-controlled territory. Bulgarian migrants paid boat captains to safely and secretly transport their families across the Prut River. In the 1820s, the Russian state's efforts to improve and strengthen its quarantine and customs lines along the Prut River were geared, in part, towards checking illicit commercial and migratory traffic. As noted in official Russian reports of the time, this kind of activity picked up considerably in the early part of the 19th century. In the second half of the 19th century and into the early part of the 20th, large numbers of Russian Muslim pilgrims traveled illegally (i.e. without passports) across the Black Sea to the Holy Lands of Mecca and Medina, and remained outside the effective control of Russian imperial administration.[52] Of the 10,000 Caucasian pilgrims reported to have accompanied the 1885 Damascus *Hajj* caravan, only 500 possessed Russian imperial pilgrimage passports.[53] Arabian agents and guides operating in Odessa and Istanbul assisted Russian pilgrims in evading Russian *Hajj* regulations.[54]

These kinds of illicit activities and practices continue to occur in the Black Sea region today. Arms and contraband are smuggled across the porous Moldovan-Ukrainian border and through the Black Sea port of Odessa.[55] The Black Sea region is notorious for human trafficking and forced prostitution.[56] Odessa and Trabzon (on the southern or Turkish Black Sea coast) act as important hubs for this modern-day slave trade. These smuggling and human-trafficking networks operate within and take advantage of the significant north-south migratory dynamic in the Black Sea region.[57] Rising income inequality between post-Soviet states (notably Russia, Ukraine, and Moldova) and Turkey foster this north-south migration flow, as does the relatively lax visa regime in Turkey for tourists and travelers from post-Soviet states. While 85 percent of Moldovan applicants for Schengen-zone passports are rejected, a citizen of Moldova need only pay US$10 at a Turkish border crossing post to gain entry into Turkey.[58]

The north-south migration dynamic in the Black Sea region is sustained by information disseminated via formal and informal communication networks maintained by migrant diaspora communities in the Black Sea basin. Smugglers, human traffickers, and recruiters prey upon vulnerable young women in Moldova and Ukraine susceptible to stories and rumors of a better life in Turkey. While many young people from post-Soviet states in the Black Sea region migrate to Turkey in search of jobs typical of unskilled labor migrants around the globe (domestic work, caregiving, bartending, waitressing, and construction work), human trafficking and the forcible recruitment of young women into the sex-for-pay industry is a tragic consequence of migratory circulation in the Black Sea region. By most estimates, the sex-for-pay industry in Turkey is a multi-billion-dollar business. A good "worker" can earn a trafficker up to US$2,000 per day.[59] Sexual slavery in the Black Sea region takes many forms, from forced prostitution to pay off debts incurred during the period of migration, to outright bondage and captivity (with reports of young women from Moldova and Ukraine forced to service 10–40 clients per day). Moldova and Ukraine are the two main source countries for victims of sexual trafficking in the Black Sea region.

Throughout the modern history of the Black Sea region, illegal and clandestine population movements around the Black Sea basin have engendered, through the coordination of efforts and the pooling of resources, the state-driven and/or technically oriented variant of Black Sea regionalism. The BSEC has assumed a regional mandate to check transnational criminal activities. Interior ministry representatives from Black Sea countries meet annually to coordinate efforts to combat organized crime, illegal trafficking of drugs and arms, terrorism, corruption, and money laundering. At the level of implementation, these efforts are coordinated through the Black Sea Police Liaison Center in Istanbul.[60]

The anti-crime and anti-trafficking efforts of the BSEC are supported by the IOM, which advocates a regional response to criminal activity. IOM's regional efforts include the promotion of dialogue among Black Sea states to manage migration effectively as a counter to transnational organized crime; the distribution of fliers on human trafficking in airports, seaports, train stations, and bus stations around the Black Sea littoral; the establishment of a hotline for victims of prostitution and sexual slavery; and the training of border guards, customs officials, law enforcement officers, police, and military personnel on migration issues.[61] IOM's regional consultative process brings together representatives of states, international organizations, and some nongovernmental organizations (NGOs) for informal and nonbinding dialogue and information exchange on migration-related issues of common interest and concern. In the Black Sea region and elsewhere, IOM operates under the premise that "regional and inter-regional approaches allow for the best opportunity for concrete and practical outcomes than global discussions."[62]

New Trajectories in Contemporary Black Sea Regionalism

Environmentalism

The forces of globalization have produced new forms of regional alliance and cooperation. Foremost among them is the adoption of regional approaches to deal with transnational environmental issues. In the early 1990s, individual American states coordinated efforts with Canadian provinces in the Great Lakes region of North America to curb the regional proliferation of acid rain. In North America, this regional approach to transnational environmental problems has persisted into the early 21st century. Oregon, Washington state, and the Canadian province of British Columbia (sometimes referred to collectively as "Cascadia") have together undertaken cooperative ventures to manage transnational water use, reduce pollution in the transboundary Seattle-Vancouver region, and link wind-generated power and distribution networks.[63] Currently, the United Nations Environment Programme (UNEP) acts as the secretariat for a dozen or so regional pollution agreements covering the Caribbean Sea, East Africa, the Arab Maghreb, and South Asia. The continued development of environmental consciousness and a more serious understanding of the consequences of long-term global climate change will continue to necessitate the adoption of regional solutions, both in the Black Sea region and around the world.

Starting in the mid-19th century, environmental scientists were among the first to conceptualize and promote an understanding of the Black Sea region as a discrete and integrated unit of exchange and interaction. Building on ideas in the discipline of ecology, these scholars conceived of the region as a web of connections and networks. Within this organic complex, they argued, changes occurring in one part of the organism necessarily impacted the health and vitality of other parts. According to Charles King, these individuals "were among the first to treat the Black Sea as a unit of study, a complex system that had to be understood as a whole through an analysis of its geography, geology, chemistry, and biology."[64]

In the contemporary Black Sea region the most developed and effective regional initiatives can be found in the field of environmental protection. Notionally, political and civic leaders in the littoral states understand that environmental issues are most effectively dealt with at the regional level. The need to arrive at a regional solution to protect the region's natural and economic resources is clear. Beaches need to be clean in order to promote tourism. The sea needs to be free of pollution to sustain fishing industries and create jobs. In this sense, regionally based environmental activism and the sense of a shared stewardship of maritime resources acts as a counter to the mutually assured degradation attendant with the "tragedy of the commons."[65]

In 1992, the six states of the Black Sea littoral signed a convention "On the Protection of the Black Sea against Pollution" (otherwise known as the "Bucharest Convention"). This convention established the Black Sea Environmental Program (BSEP).[66] Under the auspices of the BSEP, a baseline report on environmental conditions in the Black Sea region was issued in 1995, and a variety of reports and surveys have subsequently appeared on an annual basis. These reports identify various regional threats to the ecosystem of the Black Sea, including industrial pollution, pesticides, oil spills, radioactive byproducts, and wastewater discharge, and highlight the decades of environmental inattentiveness that resulted in the diminution of biodiversity in the Black Sea basin. In these reports, the Black Sea is considered, from an ecological perspective, as a single, integrated system and the economic motives (from sustainable tourism, to aquaculture, to job creation) for cleaning up the sea and its shores are stressed. In a paean to regionality and regional cooperation, the reports argue that in order to establish effective conservation measures, stakeholders must be prepared to cede sovereignty to regional mechanisms, "irrespective of national boundaries."[67]

A close reading of these environmental surveys indicates that the countries of the Black Sea region have made significant progress over the past decade, collectively and at a regional level, in reversing environmental degradation in the Black Sea basin.[68] Conservation areas have been identified and prioritized according to their regional importance, with significant efforts made to protect them. Wetlands have been stabilized, resulting in the return of migratory waterfowl. Regional wastewater treatment plants and sewer systems have been upgraded. And overfishing has been addressed.[69]

The discourse and dynamics of environmentalism in the Black Sea region have spawned a variety of social movements, most prominently environmental or ecologically focused NGOs. The Cooperative Marine Science Programme for the Black Sea is comprised of a group of scientists, marine biologists, and environmental engineers from the six littoral countries of the Black Sea and is dedicated to "the establishment of a scientific basis for the effective and integrated management of the Black Sea, including environmental preservation, protection, and optimum utilization." The Danube River Basin Programme is composed of a mix of government representatives and NGOs who are collectively devoted to "institutional strengthening, capacity building, NGO activities, water quality monitoring, data collection and assessment, accidental warning systems, pre-investment activities, applied research, and the preparation of a 'Danube River Basin Strategic Action Plan.'" Every year on October 31 (the date of the signing of the Strategic Action Plan on the Protection and Rehabilitation of the Black Sea in 1996), the countries of the Black Sea region celebrate International Black Sea Day by staging community-involvement and awareness-raising activities, and distributing materials concerning the environmental protection of the Black Sea and its resources.

The recent and coordinated protests staged by thousands of villagers along the Turkish Black Sea coast against the high levels of pollution emitted from antiquated power plants provide further evidence of the continued development of civil society in the six littoral Black Sea states. Coupled with increasing support and advocacy among nongovernmental actors and organizations for sustainable development, these developments will encourage the forward impetus of environmentally oriented regionalism. Social movements challenge sovereignty, transcend hierarchies, cross borders, promote regional cooperation, and bridge political divides. In their valorization of the environment above politics, security, or national boundaries Black Sea-based environmental movements resemble the redemptive societies identified by Prasenjit Duara in the context of late 19th- and early 20th-century pan-Asianism. These redemptive societies placed regional or civilizational loyalty above allegiance to the nation-state and, as part of what Duara terms "transnational spiritualism," respected nature and worked to counter greed, strife, and warfare.[70]

For individuals and communities in the Black Sea basin, regional participation and/or the adoption of a regional identity provides an outlet for non-state-sponsored activism as well as a competing (and potentially safe) forum to question and criticize state policies. As the Black Sea Commission cogently argued in its *2020 Vision for the Black Sea Region*, the principles of sustainable development should be "the guiding philosophy of regional cooperation in the Black Sea area. In this way, we should seek to restore and preserve a rational and enduring equilibrium between economic development and the integrity of the natural environment in ways that society can understand and accept. Rational responses to the consequences of climate change and the responsible use of natural, human, and societal resources are essential components of such a development model, which should be translated into coherent policies at national and regional level."[71]

Extra-Regional Security Interests in the Black Sea Region

Operating on a different track from socially and civically oriented forces of regional integration, *extra*-regional forces and the influence of international regimes in the Black Sea region have the potential to both disrupt and promote the emergence of politically oriented forms of Black Sea regionalism. The European Union professes to a panoply of political- and security-related interests in the Black Sea region. Over the course of the last decade, EU interests in the Black Sea region have focused on energy security, migration management, and border control in southeastern Europe; the suppression of organized crime in the Black Sea region; and the region's role in the "war on terror."

Energy security is among the top priorities for the European Union and its member-states. Currently, Russia provides approximately a quarter of the natural gas consumed in the European Union, and an even larger percentage of the natural gas and oil consumed in the European Union is imported through Russian-controlled pipelines. The Ukrainian gas crisis of January 2006 served as a wake-up call to the EU on the perils of remaining energy dependent on the Russian Federation. In January 2006, a long-simmering dispute between Russia and Ukraine over the price of natural gas and transit costs prompted Russia to cut off natural gas supplies through Ukrainian pipelines. This and subsequent disruptions resulted in a severe winter shortage in natural gas supplies in 18 European Union countries.

Over the last few years, therefore, key EU member-states have begun to look upon the wider Black Sea region as an important alternate source of energy and have made concerted efforts to construct and control the east-west pipelines across the Black Sea region that tap into the extensive hydrocarbon resources of the Caspian basin. The importance of hydrocarbon energy security in Europe is set to increase as several European countries (including Germany) have, in the wake of the 2011 nuclear crisis in Japan, signaled their intention to curtail the construction of nuclear power stations. Additionally, the Polish government made external energy security, and the question of Europe's dependence on Russian gas, one of the main agenda items during the Polish presidency of the European Union in the second half of 2011.[72] EU-Russian friction in the wake of Euro-Atlantic initiatives to reduce dependency on Russian-sourced and transported energy supplies will continue to divide the countries of the Black Sea region into shifting Russian and Euro-Atlantic spheres of influence.

The Black Sea region is a focal point for many of the irregular migration routes leading into Europe. Two of the main east-west routes are the Balkan Route, flowing from the Middle East through Turkey, Bulgaria, and Romania into central Europe, and the eastern Mediterranean route, which uses Greece as its access point to the Schengen passport-free zone.[73] In the last few years, the Greek-Turkish border (along the Evros River) has become the primary illegal route for immigrants entering Europe, surpassing Spain and Italy. In 2010, an estimated 47,000 migrants crossed from Turkey into Greece, and overall annual immigration into Greece is estimated, over the last few years, to have topped 80,000. In the first four months of 2014, migrant arrivals increased 140 percent, with the majority of this increase due to the intensification of the civil war in Syria.[74] Border-control mechanisms in Greece remain weak, and migrant and asylee processing slow and susceptible to corruption. Human traffickers therefore maintain an active and visible presence along the Greek-Turkish border. Most illegal migrants crossing the Greek-Turkish border come from Afghanistan, Iran, Pakistan, and Somalia.[75] In 2010, chronic corruption along Romania's porous border prompted the Romanian government to arrest 248 border and customs officials, many of whom were accused of pocketing about EUR 5,800 per shift.[76] A renewed outbreak of hostilities in any of the "frozen" conflicts in the wider Black Sea region (principally in Transnistria, or in Abkhazia and Ossetia in Georgia), coming as it would on the heels of the admission of Bulgaria and Romania into the Schengen passport-free zone, would only increase migratory pressure on the European Union's eastern and southeastern borders with Russia and the Middle East. The level of stress placed on Europe's external and internal migration regimes would resemble the pressures faced by the European Union in the wake of increased migratory and refugee flows from North Africa and the Middle East into southern Europe produced by the Arab Spring and subsequent turmoil in the Greater Middle East.

Security analysts in Europe and the United States have detected a convergence of illicit trafficking and smuggling activities around the Black Sea, and have uncovered connections between large organized-crime syndicates and terrorist networks in the Black Sea region. Collectively, the activities and connections of these groups and networks have produced what is known in national security parlance as "non-traditional security threats." In 2003, the US Department of Justice identified Semyon Mogilevich as the head of a Black Sea criminal gang of over 300 active members. According to the justice department, Mogilevich's gang engaged in murder, extortion, trafficking in women for prostitution, smuggling, money laundering, bank and securities fraud, and the corruption of public officials in the Black Sea region.[77]

As a group of US experts on international organized crime and terrorism have noted, frozen conflicts in the Black Sea region create "numerous opportunities for the growth of organized crime and terrorism." Feeding on the erosion of government authority and the weakness of the rule of law in Black Sea countries, transnational criminal and terrorist networks have exploited the region's political and security vacuum. Long-standing east-west trading connections (on both land and sea) across the historical crossroads of the Black Sea region have provided key transportation routes for the illicit movement of goods and cargo, and the transport links are shared by terrorist outfits and criminal gangs. Falsified passports and the corruption of border guards ease movements across national borders. Rebels in Ossetia have morphed into criminal gangs. Revenue generated by cigarette sales, drug sales, and arms smuggling finance terrorist groups: the Black Sea region is the key transit route for Afghan heroin entering the European market. In short, according to US and European experts, the interaction between terrorism and organized crime in the Black Sea region is "more pronounced than in most other regions of the world due to the significant number of ethnic conflicts, the density of criminal and terrorist groups in the region, and the region's strategic geographic location."[78] Going forward, these security-related factors will continue to validate extra-regional intervention in the region's affairs.

While regionalisms, regional identities, and regional interaction draw largely upon older or structural and internal drivers of regional cohesion, they can also react to and owe their emergence to developments and stimuli from outside the region. The re-appearance of extra-regional regimes in the early part of the 21st century could provoke a defensive and regionally expressed Russian-Turkish response to outside interference in the political affairs of the Black Sea region. Drawing upon historical roots, the re-establishment of a Russian-Turkish condominium over the Black Sea could galvanize state-driven efforts to deepen the economic and political integration of the Black Sea region, as it did in the late 18th and early 19th centuries.

The impulse among the states, societies, and peoples of the Black Sea region towards enhanced participation in Black Sea forums and organizations could be driven by perceptions of and antipathy towards Euro-Atlantic "upper-classism."[79] Russia's disapproving postimperial attitude towards the Euro-Atlantic world is well documented and has been put into practice in

Crimea and eastern Ukraine. Rising populism and xenophobia in European politics, coupled with the obstructionism of key EU members (such as France) has curtailed, for the time being, talk of Turkish accession to the EU. Georgian efforts to get in line for EU (and NATO) admission have been re buffed, and the recent signing of Georgian free-trade agreement with the EU notwithstanding, remain highly contingent. And the future geopolitical bearing of Ukraine is, of course, very much up in the air. To quote the American and European authors of a study on European interests in the region, "aspirations to EU membership by countries like Ukraine, Moldova or the South Caucasus will for the foreseeable future be met in Brussels with silence at best or cold rejection at worst."[80]

Even the current EU members Bulgaria and Romania chafe at the pressure applied by Brussels to tighten regulations on food and alcohol production and distribution, enact judicial reforms, eliminate corruption, and crack down on organized crime. This friction is no doubt exacerbated by the very public admission of some leading Eurocrats that Bulgaria and Romania were allowed into the EU club too soon. In an echo of 19th- and 20th-century geopolitical alignments, any increase or uptick in Bulgarian resentment towards the European Union raises the possibility (after a rather short "European Spring") of Bulgaria's return to Russia's political orbit.

As Rebecca Karl writes, "shared experiences of oppression" have historically led peoples "to construct for themselves global blocs that were independent of existing states and incipient regional formations, and that allowed them to link up for radical political purposes and to construct regional solidarities out of their perceived global structural commonality."[81] Indeed, regionalism can act as a counter to, or a displacer of, would-be hegemonic states and ideologies. This political dynamic has occurred throughout the history of the Black Sea region. In the early part of the 20th century, exiled anti-Bolshevik leaders from those Black Sea states that had been absorbed into the Soviet Union (Georgia, Azerbaijan, Ukraine, and Crimea) formed a movement that Charles King believes "represented the first modern attempt to think about the Black Sea as a distinct political unit."[82] Conceived of in opposition to Soviet ideological and geopolitical hegemony in the Black Sea region, this movement (known as the Promethean project) called for the creation of a political and economic alliance of "free" Black Sea states including Bulgaria, Romania, and Turkey. With this historical example as a template, it is plausible that going forward Turkey and Russia could formulate a vision of Black Sea regionalism crafted around an alliance of Black Sea states organized in opposition to incipient Euro-Atlantic hegemony over political, military, and economic affairs in the region.

Conclusion: Challenges and Prospects for the Field of Regionalism

Accoording to Charles King, "at various points in history a distinct region defined by the Black Sea and its hinterlands has been a commonplace of European affairs, although the limits of that region have fluctuated over time."[83] This manuscript has argued that the factors which helped the Black Sea region achieve historical specificity in the late 18th and early 19th centuries (Russian-Turkish condominium over political and economic affairs in the Black Sea region and increased human mobility) are re-emerging and that this re-emergent regionality will have economic, political, and security-related implications for societies and states within and without the Black Sea region. External regimes (principally NATO and the European Union) will continue to impact the contours and depth of Black Sea regionalism. For example, despite the fact that the Black Sea region is currently bifurcated between states within and without these international regimes, it is plausible that external pressures could provoke a regionalist reaction led by the two most powerful Black Sea states (Russia and Turkey) and supported by states frustrated by the nature and tone of their Euro-Atlantic relations. In sum, the combination of historical factors (the re-emergence of a Russian-Turkish duopoly over Black Sea affairs) and contemporary realties (weakness in both NATO and the European Union) leads to speculation that we could be entering a particularly robust (and turbulent) period in the history Black Sea regionalism.

The conceptual principles of the burgeoning and potentially influential field of regionalism have the ability to assist analysts and educators in tracking and making sense of ongoing economic, political, and cultural developments in the Black Sea region. For this goal to be reached, however, several challenges inherent in the study of regions will have to be met. I believe it is not helpful (especially when looking at a young or "newish," post-1990 regional expression such as the Black Sea region) to elide empirically based studies of regionalism in favor of overly theoretical discussions on the ways in which regions are constructed or imagined. One problematic here, perhaps, is the need to develop tools to measure more precisely the connectivity and resonance (economically, politically, and culturally) of regionalism and regional formations on the quotidian needs and interests of societies and peoples in the region under scrutiny. An increased focus by scholars on the technical dimensions of regionalism should help in this regard. In the context of the Black Sea region the elaboration of measurable benchmarks in the areas of environmentalism, economic relations, regional infrastructure projects, and Black Sea tourism would guide scholars in gauging the depth and pace of technical and institutional regionalism in the context of the Black Sea region.[84]

I concur with most analyses of Black Sea regionalism that in the post-Cold War era regional formation in the Black Sea region has primarily been a state-constructed and state-sponsored enterprise. However, at the grassroots (or popular) level one can detect forces that are in the business of de-emphasizing the saliency of the state in the Black Sea region. Human mobility will continue to drive the process of regional formation in the Black Sea basin. Historically, regions have been "constructed" not only through state-sponsored projects but through a more organic or natural process animated by regionally bound cultural mobility. Indeed, the development of analytical tools to track and detect the linkages (and potential convergence of) state-constructed regional formations with the organic and historically grounded dynamics of socially and environmentally generated regionalism will establish and extend the intellectual impact of the field of regional studies.

In the early 21st century there is a very real tendency towards regional crystallizations in the world system. Going forward the twin forces of regionalism and globalization will, more than likely, continue to erode the sovereignty of the nation-state. Inherent in this dynamic is the potential for a cleavage between regionalism and globalization. This rupture will be caused by the stimulation of what Leo Ching has termed the individual, communal, and social "cravings for fixity and locality within the transience of globalization."[85] It is here that the intellectual and ideological power of regionalism lies. Regional dynamics can have more meaning (in the sense of their localness) and can have more resonance for individuals and societies (and perhaps even states) than ethereal global forces. Regional formations will be strong competitors for the political and/or cultural allegiance of the transnationally conscious citizens of the 21st-century world.

Notes

1. For more on the "closing" of the Black Sea under the Ottomans in the early modern period, see Carl M. Kortepeter, "Ottoman Imperial Policy and the Economy of the Black Sea Region in the Sixteenth Century," *Journal of the American Oriental Society* 86, no. 2 (April–June 1966): 86–113.

2. Early 19th-century travelers in the Black Sea region drew the same conclusions. For example, the French traveler John Baron de Reuilly noted in 1803 the existence of a Black Sea zone of commercial exchange and maintained that international trading links with the Black Sea were being made "in the same manner as in the times of the Genoese." John Baron de Reuilly, *Travels in the Crimea and Along the Shores of the Black Sea Performed during the Year 1803* (London: Richard Phillips, 1807), 6.

3. Charles King, "Is the Black Sea a Region?" in *The Black Sea Region: Cooperation and Security Building*, ed. Oleksander Pavliuk and Ivana Klympush-Tsintsadze (London: M.E. Sharpe, 2004), 19–20.

4. The force and efficacy of "regional cooperation" is based on the assumption that every country in a regional formation benefits more from collective action than as an independent actor. A plausible model for enhanced Black Sea regionalism could be recent initiatives by Central American states to promote regional integration through planned regional projects, the creation of regional rapporteur to monitor the implementation of regional directives, and the diversion of international aid and loans away from individual countries towards regional efforts. "Security in Central America: Rounding up the Governments," *The Economist*, June 25, 2011, 47–48.

5. Of the total Black Sea shoreline of 4340 km, Ukraine covers 1628 km, Turkey covers 1400 km, Russia covers 475 km, Georgia covers 310 km, Bulgaria covers 300 km, and Romania covers 225 km.

6. International Organization for Migration, *Migration in the Black Sea Region: An Overview 2008* (Geneva: IOM, 2008), 9.

7. Charles King, "The Wider Black Sea Region in the 21st Century," in *The Wider Black Sea Region in the 21st Century: Strategic, Economic,*

and Energy Perspectives, ed. Daniel Hamilton and Gerhard Mangott (Washington, DC: Center for Transatlantic Relations, 2008), 1.

8. For example, in convening a roundtable of regional leaders from government, business, academia, multilateral organizations, and civil society to discuss the prevention and settlement of conflict in the Black Sea region, the East-West Institute invited participants from the littoral Black Sea states *and* Armenia, Azerbaijan, and Moldova. As an example of the deleterious impact that Greek and Turkish membership can have on regional relations, Greece recently vetoed Montenegro's accession to BSEC in retaliation for Turkey's veto of the proposed accession of Cyprus to the BSEC.

9. Pertti Joenniemi, "Regionality: A Sovereign Principle of International Relations?" in *Peaceful Changes in World Politics,* Research Report 71, ed. Heikki Patomaki (Tampere, Finland: Tampere Peace Research Institute, 1995), 338–73.

10. Rebecca E. Karl, "Creating Asia: China in the World at the Beginning of the 20th Century," *American Historical Review* 103, no. 4 (October 1998): 1114.

11. It may be worth mentioning here that 20 years after the dissolution of the Soviet Union the future composition and viability of the NATO alliance is very much in doubt. As former US Secretary of Defense Robert Gates remarked, unless European countries assume more of NATO's defense and military burden, the Euro-Atlantic alliance faces "collective military irrelevance" and a "dim and dismal future." "Charlemagne: On Target," *The Economist,* June 18, 2011, 62.

12. Inspired by Fernand Braudel's magisterial work on the Mediterranean Sea, the Black Sea has of late received Braudel-like treatment from Western scholars as well as from scholars in various Black Sea countries. The list of the historical works on the Black Sea region undertaken by European, American, and Black Sea-based scholars includes Charles King, *The Black Sea: A History* (New York: Oxford University Press, 2004); Neal Ascherson, *Black Sea* (New York: Hill and Wang, 1995); Halil Inalcık, "The Question of the Closing of the Black Sea under the Ottomans" *Archeion Pontou* 33 (1979): 75–100; Aleksander Halenko, "Towards the Character of Ottoman Policy in the Northern Black Sea Region after the Treaty of Belgrade (1739)," *Oriente Moderno* 18, no. 1 (1999): 101–13; Victor Ostapchuk, "The Human Landscape of the Ottoman Black Sea in the Face of the Cossack Naval Raids," *Oriente Moderno* 20, no. 1 (2001): 23–95; Velko Tonev, *Bulgarskoto Chernomorie Prez Vuzrazhdaneto* (Sofia, Bulgaria: Akademichno Izdatelstvo "Prof. Marin Drinov," 1995); *Bulgarite v Severnoto*

Prichernomorie: Izsledvaniia i Materiali, 4 vol. (Veliko Tarnovo, Bulgaria: Velikoturnovski universitet "Sv. sv. Kiril i Metodii," 1992–95); Elena Druzhinina, *Severnoe Prichernomor'e, 1775–1800* (Moscow: Izdatelstvo Nauka, 1959); and Idris Bostan "Izn-i Sefine Defterleri ve Karadenize Rusya ile Ticaret Yapan Devlet-i Aliyye Tüccarlari, 1780–1846," *Türklük Araştırmaları Dergisi* 6 (1990): 21–41.

13. King, "Is the Black Sea a Region?" 15.

14. Eyüp Özveren, "A Framework for the Study of the Black Sea World, 1789–1915," *Review of the Fernand Braudel Center* 20, no. 1 (Winter 1997): 92.

15. Here I am drawing upon arguments made by Rebecca Karl in the context of early 20th-century Asianism. Karl, "Creating Asia," 1117.

16. This is an argument that Andrew Gamble and Anthony Payne have made about regionalism in general. See Andrew Gamble and Anthony Payne, eds., *Regionalism and World Order* (New York: St. Martin's Press, 1996).

17. Commission on the Black Sea, *A 2020 Vision for the Black Sea Region* (May 17, 2010), 23. According to the preface, this group aims "to contribute to a joint vision and a common strategy for the Black Sea region by developing new knowledge in areas of key concern. As existing research tends to focus on specific topics, for example energy, transport or the environment and is mostly viewed from one-sided national or western and Euro-Atlantic perspectives, the Commission aims to redress this imbalance by developing a comprehensive, policy-oriented study jointly with scholars and stakeholders from the region as well as from countries outside the Black Sea area, with a view to being as objective and balanced as possible. The goal is to present not just short-term, sectoral or stakeholder-specific interests, but to provide input for a new vision and long-term strategy for the Black Sea region." *2020 Vision*, 27.

18. I have adopted the concept of a "supranational regional imaginary" and the concept of regionalist culture from Leo Ching, "Globalizing the Regional, Regionalizing the Global: Mass Culture and Asianism in the Age of Late Capital," *Public Culture* 12 (2000): 238–39. According to Ching, "whereas material exchanges tend to foster ties to localities and political exchanges tend to foster ties to territory, symbolic exchanges liberate relationships from spatial referents."

19. Karl, "Creating Asia," 1109.

20. Özveren, "Framework for the Study," 96.

21. Özveren, "Framework for the Study," 83.

22. By 1897, Muslims accounted for 11 percent of the Russian Empire's population. Andreas Kappeler, *Russland als Vielvölkerreich* (Munich: Verlag C.H. Beck, 1993), 234. The Muslim population of the late 19th century was roughly 10 million. The incorporation of the Khanates of Bukhara, Samarkand, and Khiva alone brought five million Muslims within the Russian Empire. Daniel Brower, "Russian Roads to Mecca: Religious Tolerance and Muslim Pilgrimage in the Russian Empire," *Slavic Review* 55, no. 3 (1996): 569. One scholar estimates that the Muslim population of the Russian Empire at the end of the 19th century was closer to 18 million. R.G. Landa, *Islam v Istorii Rossii* (Moscow: Vostochnaia Literatura, 1995), 107.

23. Brower, "Russian Roads to Mecca," 574–75.

24. Kemal Karpat, "The *Hijra* from Russia and the Balkans," in *Muslim Travellers: Pilgrimage, Migration, and the Religious Imagination,* ed. Dale Eickelman and James Piscatori (Berkeley: University of California Press, 1990), 133–34.

25. Zavdat S. Minnullin, "Fraternal and Benevolent Associations of Tatar Students in Muslim Countries at the Beginning of the 20th Century," in *Muslim Culture in Russia and Central Asia from the 18th to the Early 20th Centuries, vol. II, ed.* Michael Kemper, Anke von Kügelgen, and Dmitriy Yermakov (Berlin: Klaus Schwarz Verlag, 1996), 275.

26. A.G. Karimullin, *Tatarskaia Kniga Nachala XX Veka* (Kazan: Tatarskoe kn. izd-vo, 1974), 220–23.

27. Brower, "Russian Roads to Mecca," 567.

28. King, *The Black Sea*, 191.

29. Brian Williams, *The Crimean Tatars* (Boston: Brill, 2001), 182.

30. *Hürriyet*, May 14, 2010.

31. *Hürriyet*, May 14, 2010.

32. A negotiated settlement between Azerbaijan and Armenia over the future disposition of Nagorno-Karabakh would remove one of the few remaining points of geo-political tension between Russia and Turkey in the Black Sea region.

33. Fisher, "Emigration of Muslims," 357.

34. Williams, *The Crimean Tatars,* 109. Mark Pinson estimates that 30,000–40,000 Crimean Tatars left the Russian Empire for the Ottoman Empire during the Crimean War and that an additional 100,000 Crimean

Tatar and 50,000 Nogay Tatar refugees fled the Russian Empire in 1860 and 1861. Mark Pinson, "Russian Policy and the Emigration of the Crimean Tatars to the Ottoman Empire, 1854–1862," in *Güney-Doğu Avrupa Araştırmaları Dergisi* (Istanbul: Edebiyat Fakültesi Basimevi, 1972), 44, 47.

35. James H. Meyer, "Immigration, Return, and the Politics of Citizenship: Russian Muslims in the Ottoman Empire, 1860–1914," *International Journal of Middle East Studies* 39, no. 1 (February 2007): 15.

36. Kemal Karpat, "Muslim Migration: A Response to Adeeb Abu-Sahlieh," *International Migration Review* 30, no. 1 (1996): 87. Mark Pinson estimates that between 1855 and 1866, 1,000,000 Circassian refugees fled from the Caucasus to the Ottoman Empire. 600,000 of these Circassian refugees were settled in the Balkans and the remaining 400,000 settled in Anatolia. Mark Pinson, "Ottoman Colonization of the Circassians in Rumuli after the Crimean War," *Études Balkaniques* 3 (1972): 75. Alan Fisher estimates that the total number of Tatars and Circassians who fled the Russian Empire between 1856 and 1862 was 700,000–900,000. Alan Fisher, "Emigration of Muslims from the Russian Empire in the Years after the Crimean War," *Jahrbücher für Geschicte Osteuropas* 35 (1987): 364.

37. King, *The Black Sea*, 211.

38. To learn more about the events of this period in the demographic history of the Black Sea region, see Justin McCarthy, *Death and Exile: the Ethnic Cleansing of Ottoman Muslims, 1821–1922* (Princeton, NJ: Darwin Press, 1995) and Stefan Doinov, *Bulgarite v Ukraina i Moldova prez Vuzrazhdaneto, 1751–1878* (Sofia, Bulgaria: Akademichno Izdatelstvo "Prof. Marin Drinov," 2005).

39. Ivan Meshcheriuk, *Pereselenie Bolgar v Iuzhnuiu Besarabiiu 1828–1834 gg.* (Kishinev: 1965), 196–97.

40. Meyer, "Immigration, Return," 24.

41. Meyer, "Immigration, Return," 28.

42. "Doklad na Logofeta Sht. Vlŭdesku do Izpŭlnitelniia Divan vŭv Vrŭska s Preminavaneto i Nastaniavaneto na Bŭlgarski Bezhantsi" (May 23, 1830), *Bŭlgarite v Rumŭnia, XVII–XX v.: Dokumenti i Materiali*, comp. and ed. Maxim Mladenov, Nikolai Zhechev, and Blagovest Niagulov (Sofia: Akademichno Izdatelstvo "Marin Drinov," 1994), 27–28.

43. "Molba na 49 Bŭlgarski Semeistva ot Selo Sloboziia do General Kiselov za Osvobozhdane ot Danutsi kato Postradali ot Voinata" (January 9, 1832), *Bŭlgarite v Rumŭnia, XVII–XX v.: Dokumenti i Materiali*, 43–44.

44. Iov Titorov, *Bulgarite v Bessarabia* (Sofia: 1903), 28.

45. Kemal Karpat, "Ottoman Urbanism: The Crimean Emigration to Dobruca and the Founding of Mecidiye, 1856–1878," in *Studies on Ottoman Social and Political History* (Boston: Brill, 2002), 13–15.

46. For more on this topic see my article "The Danube Vilayet and the Bulgar-Turkish Compromise Proposal of 1867 in Bulgarian Historiography," *International Journal of Turkish Studies* 14, no. 1–2 (Fall 2008): 61–74.

47. For more on the Greek diaspora community in Odessa see Viron Karidis, "A Greek Mercantile Paroikia: Odessa, 1774–1829," in *Balkan Society in the Age of Greek Independence,* ed. Richard Clogg (Totowa, NJ: Barnes and Noble Books, 1981), 111–36.

48. IOM, *Migration in the Black Sea Region,* 52–60.

49. IOM, *Migration in the Black Sea Region,* 52–60.

50. In general, in the last decade of the 18th century and the first part of the 19th century, Russian state servitors engaged in a pro-active "international" campaign to identify, recruit, and transport migrant-settlers from Ottoman Rumelia and the Danubian Principalities to the sparsely populated lands of southern Russia and Bessarabia. It should be noted, however, that the promotion of continuous refugee and migrant resettlement from the Ottoman Empire to the Russian Empire was not a blanket Russian state policy during the period in question. Periodically, statesmen in Saint Petersburg—as part of Russian diplomatic initiatives to improve relations with the Ottoman Empire—ordered the curtailment of migrant recruitment and removal operations in the Danubian Principalities and Ottoman Rumelia. V.P. Grachev, "Kŭm Vŭprosa za Preselvaneto na Bŭlgari v Rusiia v Nachaloto na XIX v., 1800-1806 g.," *Bŭlgarskoto Vŭzrazhdane i Rusiia* (Sofia: "Nauka i Izkustvo," 1981), 276–77. The Russian historian Elena Druzhinina notes that in the period after the annexation of the Crimea, "Turkish agents" and "Turkish spies" were active on the peninsula. According to Druzhinina, these agents engaged in clandestine "smuggling operations." Plying the Crimean coast at night, boats manned by Ottoman spies took on Crimean Tatar migrants and brought them to safety in the Ottoman Empire. Druzhinina, *Severnoe Prichernomor'e,* 99, 119.

51. Charles King, *The Moldovans: Romania, Russia, and the Politics of Culture* (Stanford, CA: Hoover Institution Press, 2000), 23.

52. Thomas Sanders, Ernest Tucker, and Gary Hamburg, eds., *Russian-Muslim Confrontation in the Caucasus* (London: Routledge, 2004), 176.

53. Brower, "Russian Roads to Mecca," 570, 572.

54. Hafez Farmayan and Elton Daniel, eds., *A Shi'ite Pilgrimage to Mecca, 1885–1886: The Safarnâmeh of Mirzâ Mohammad Hosayn Farâhâni* (Austin: University of Texas Press, 1990), 184.

55. Louise I. Shelley et al., *Methods and Motives: Exploring Links between Transnational Organized Crime & International Terrorism* (Rockville, MD: National Institute of Justice, 2005), 65–66.

56. The Bulgarian-born journalist and filmmaker Mimi Chakarova has recently produced *The Price of Sex*, a riveting, shocking, and highly educational documentary film on human trafficking and prostitution in the Black Sea region. Within the framework of regional migration, Chakarova explores the transnational causes and regional networks that have contributed to the proliferation of human trafficking and forced migration in the Black Sea region.

57. In 2004, roughly 2.7 million tourists from the former Soviet Union visited Turkey. In 2009, 2.6 million tourists from Russia alone travelled to Turkey. This number increased to over 3 million in 2010 and is projected to reach 5 million by 2015—surpassing Germany as the main country of origin for tourists travelling to Turkey (the number of annual tourists from Germany to Turkey is currently around 4 million). East-West Institute, *Regional and Transfrontier Cooperation as a Tool for Conflict Prevention and Settlement in the Black Sea Region* (Istanbul: EWI, 2006), 6 and *Hürriyet*, May 14, 2010.

58. Marielle Sander Lindstrom, "Turkey's Efforts to Fight Human Trafficking in the Black Sea Region: A Regional Approach," *The Quarterly Journal* (Winter 2005): 42. Marielle Sander Lindstrom is a former chief of mission at the International Organization for Migration in Ankara, Turkey.

59. Sander Lindstrom, "Turkey's Efforts," 42.

60. Lada L. Roslycky, "Organized Transnational Crime in the Black Sea Region: A Geopolitical Dilemma?" *Trends in Organized Crime* 12, no. 1 (March 2009): 4 and Commission on the Black Sea, *2020 Vision*, 47.

61. Sander Lindstrom, "Turkey's Efforts," 45–47.

62. "Migration," US Department of State, http://2001-2009.state.gov/g/prm/c25775.htm.

63. Oregon's wind-generating power capacity has increased 15-fold over the past six years and one of the state's largest providers of wind-generated power is in negotiations to link this capacity to grids in British Columbia, Canada. "Tilting at Windmills: Renewable Energy in the North-West," *The Economist,* June 18, 2011, 37–38.

64. King, *The Black Sea*, 223.

65. The tragedy of the commons is a dilemma in which multiple individuals (or entities), acting independently and in accordance with their own self-interests, deplete a shared limited resource, even when it is clear that it is not in anyone's long-term interest to do so.

66. It is worth noting here that in 1974, under the auspices of the United Nations Environment Programme, Regional Seas Conventions were signed for both the Baltic and Mediterranean Seas. The Bucharest Convention of 1992 effectively acted as the Black Sea region's accession to this international mechanism.

67. Two good examples of these reports are D. Laurence Mee, *How to Save the Black Sea: Your Guide to the Black Sea Strategic Action Plan* (Istanbul: Black Sea Environmental Programme, 2001) and the Black Sea Economic Cooperation, *Ministerial Resolution on the Amendment of the Strategic Action Plan on the Rehabilitation and Protection of the Black Sea* (Sofia, Bulgaria, June 22–26, 2002).

68. An interesting sidebar to this discussion on environmental issues in the Black Sea region is the intellectual and moral role played by the Greek Orthodox Patriarchate in Istanbul. For his contributions towards raising environmental consciousness in the Black Sea region Patriarch Bartholomew as earned the sobriquet "the Green Patriarch." See Steve Bryant, "Unlikely Allies Meet to Save the Black Sea," *Reuters*, September 21, 1997.

69. King, "Wider Black Sea Region in the 21st Century," 15.

70. Prasenjit Duara, "The Discourse of Civilization and Pan-Asianism," *Journal of World History* 12, no. 1 (Spring 2001): 106–108.

71. Commission on the Black Sea, *2020 Vision*, 41.

72. "Poland and the European Union: Presidential Ambitions," *The Economist,* June 25, 2011, 66.

73. IOM, *Migration in the Black Sea Region*, 46.

74. "Tidal Wave," *The Economist,* July 15, 2014, 44.

75. "The Unstoppable Flow," *The Economist,* February 19, 2011, 60.

76. "Bloc's New Conservatism Impedes Two European Nations," *New York Times,* September 4, 2011.

77. Roslycky, "Organized Transnational Crime," 3.

78. Shelley et al., *Methods and Motives*, 64–68. See also Roslycky, "Organized Transnational Crime," 1–5.

79. I first came across the concept of European or Western "upper-classism" in Duara, "Discourse of Civilization," 101.

80. Svante Cornell et al., *The Wider Black Sea Region: An Emerging Hub in European Security* (Washington, DC: Central Asia-Caucasus Institute and the Silk Road Studies Program, 2006), 17.

81. Karl, "Creating Asia," 1114.

82. King, *The Black Sea*, 225.

83. King, "Wider Black Sea Region in the 21st Century," 2.

84. The incentive for regional cooperation in these four areas is discussed in King, "Wider Black Sea Region in the 21st Century," 18.

85. Ching, "Globalizing the Regional," 237.